Business Which Impress

The inception, hurdles and thrill of creating a world class business.

Ashenafi Bordea

Copy Right © Reserved.

Business Which Impress 1
The inception, hurdles and thrill of creating a world class business. 1

Part I - Impressive Business 4

  Chapter One - Entrepreneurial spirit. How to understand and nurture it. 5

  Chapter Two - We are in a business of selling. The customer dynamics. 36

  Chapter Three - Habits and practices for you and your company that lead to fruition. - Self Development. 72

Part II - Strong Leadership 99

  Chapter Four - Lead me to my destiny. Who is a leader? 100

  Chapter Five - The role of outs-tanding leadership in successful businesses. Impactful Leadership. 115

Part III - Vibrant Economy 135

  Chapter Six - He who defines the Economy. Economies aren't to be understood, they are to be defined. 136

  Epilogue 142

Part I - Impressive Business

Entrepreneurs have an idea and a goal as two ends of their journey. They bring an idea and make it in to being as a goal. An impressive business is what makes this possible. That is why the business of an entrepreneur is the most valuable thing in the world for him or her. He or she is usually obsessed with ways of achieving his or her goal.

Businesses which fail to impress are businesses which fail to achieve their goal. Entrepreneurs should always dare to challenge the status quo and innovate to come up with new ways of satisfying their customers. Better business practices, standardized services, amazing products are the results of impressive businesses.

Chapter One - Entrepreneurial spirit. How to understand and nurture it.

When you are equipped with the zeal and passion you have for the things you want to do in life, your entrepreneurial spirit is going to take charge. Nurturing this entrepreneurial spirit is what you should do from the beginning, therefore. It is what is going to take you from a decent and aspiring entrepreneur in to an accomplished and renowned one.

You can achieve the extraordinary with the goal you are aspiring to reach. But you may be puzzled how you are going to do it. You should start to work toward your goal from day one. If you believe in yourself, today is the day to start to do it. What you do builds up one by one.

Who is an entrepreneur? The good news and the bad news.

Entrepreneurs are risk takers. They leave aside certainty and get in to the uncertain. This will make the game very tough. But entrepreneurs are equipped with strong passion that they are always able to get past the problems they face. They emerge innovators and market leaders. The hardwork they put into their business translates in to amazing products and services which customers are going to love.

It's is hard to imagine the world without entrepreneurs. Fruits of technology and science, arts and design, or what ever we are using for that matter, reach to us, consumers, because of entrepreneurs. The dreams of entrepreneurs gave us most of the things that today seem common place but actually were impossible once.

The good news. Entrepreneurship can be learned. Entrepreneurship is a skill you may able to learn and nurture. You may turn yourself in to one of the amazing entrepreneurs the world has seen by adopting and taking lessons from them. Putting your ideas and goals into being requires that you be strong and dedicated, tough and determined.

Entrepreneurs are open minded people. They learn every bit of the things they want to do and this mindset takes them far into achieving them. They never stop learning. They are the game changers. It is therefore important that you learn the amazing traits of entrepreneurs.

The bad news, Entrepreneurship is a roller-coaster. It is very hard to decide and get into the unchartered territory. Success doesn't come easy. You have to pay the price. You are going to face setbacks and failures, ups and downs. You have to be prepared to tackle the difficulties and problems that is going to face you.

In fact all this has its own rewards. You'll come financially independent. The goal you aspired to achieve is going to pay. You'll be able to enjoy its fruits. That is why you have to stay strong emotionally. The mastery you have over the required skills, and the strength you have for winning, will take you further than you have ever imagined.

Entrepreneurial traits. The world witnessed the advance of technology we are able to see now because of entrepreneurs. The world have also witnessed amazing entrepreneurs who are able to change the world before our eyes. It is very important that we take lessons from these amazing people.

Entrepreneurs come in different forms. Adopting the traits of these successful people will make the road ahead a friendly and interesting one. We should master their traits and in fact, we should also master the good traits we uniquely have ourselves. Success is bound to happen.

This is programming 101 for entrepreneurs.

You know it happens - what you have dreamed. You know it happens - what you have thought for yourself and others. And now it is just a matter of time and attitude. How can you come up with ways of achieving your goal. It is no secret that you will come across problems. But the driving force inside you is saying it is all possible. That will enable you and empower you throughout the journey.

You won't stop to think about your goal even just for a minute. You will see doors opening, one after the other. And you see your power to win over obstacles. You will promise to never quit. And, this will give you more power and courage to continue. You will never let any opportunity pass you because of your indifference. Rather, you will seize it.

This is your chance to shine. Embrace it. You know when it is time. Now is the time. Now is the time to make your dreams come true. Now is the time to achieve your goals. This will make your next step easier. You have waited this moment for a long time. Now that you have it, you will embrace it. You will do every thing to let it happen.

Change starts to happen to you naturally. No matter how difficult it seems, you will have the ability to pass through challenges. You will have the strength to remain unshaken. Each and every steps you make takes you one step closer to your goal. The road ahead is shaped by you along the way. And you will find yourself in a place where you have always wanted.

The amazing entrepreneur. You will start to dream big. This will start to serve you. The dream you have for you and the world will take charge in your life. You will be moved by thoughts and deeds that change the world for the better. And this will bring wonders to your life. Wonders that you love to accomplish. Wonders that you will find intriguing.

You won't quit. Rather you will win. You will build inner strength to push forward. You will fall in love with life and its wonders. Achieving the extraordinary replaces mediocrity. You will be flooded with life's amazing gifts.

Programming 101 for entrepreneurs. This is like a *'Hello World'* for entrepreneurs. The urge and desire you have for changing the world leads you throughout your life. You will have an amazing attitude toward yourself and the people who dream bigger. You will be confident than you have ever been before that change is going to happen to your life.

You won't let your strength be shaken. You won't let your dream be spoiled. You will fight for it, to the furthest length. You won't quit. Rather you make the best of it. Your dream has brought you this further, and it will take you furthest to your destiny.

Choose the extraordinary rather than the ordinary. The path of an entrepreneur.

The path of an entrepreneur is the path to the extraordinary rather than the ordinary. That is why you have to follow it. There is no limit to what you are able to achieve. The thrill of taking risks, the pleasure of winning deals and customers, the euphoria of being in the driver seat, these all is going to be possible for you. It is not just amazing, it is extraordinary.

And it is you, the entrepreneur who is going to do it. You'll put everything you have in it and results are going to accrue. You won't take out your business out of your mind, not even for a minute. This will give you amazing power. You will see change not just in your life, but also in people's lives. You will see the extraordinary not just in your life, but also in people's lives.

The Extraordinary. So what is the extraordinary? Your idea is the extraordinary. Your determination and commitment is the extraordinary. Your achievements are the extraordinary. It is extraordinary because your business proved to be irresistible. It is extraordinary because your products and services proved to be amazing. It is extraordinary because the world is a better place because of you and your business.

You will be able to witness every day how what you have put forth is helping people, how you and your company are able to lead the change the world wants. Your very ambition and passion is going to give the world a surprise. Your actions and persistence is going to give the world a profit. You and your company are going to be able to take humanity forward.

You will see abundance first hand. Your company will remain to be an example and icon of change. You will be able to inspire millions. Your company will be the living memory of civilization. You will be the living legend of prosperity. Your company will have a big capital. You will be a millionaire or a billionaire. Your company will drive change. You will lead that change.

The People. So who are the people who achieve the extraordinary? These people are entrepreneurs. They are highly driven by change. They are not shy to reach the goal they set. They know they can achieve the extraordinary. So they work diligently and walk the extra mile. They know what it means to conceive a great idea and bring that in to reality.

This makes them be filled with pride. Because of their nature, they always push it to the limit. And they are usually not tricked by small successes. Rather they look for opportunities to grow their venture. They never stop to grow individually too. They challenge themselves to get to the unchartered territories. They are able to see themselves grow in all aspects of their life.

They know they are solving many questions the world needs to solve so badly. And they are moved by the change they are able to bring. That is why they never quit. That is why they are often called change agents.

Enjoy the world of Abundance.

Noble ideas are change agents. They drive change. They force change. They make every thing abundant. For each contribution you make to the world, there is a huge reward that comes to you. That reward is unlimited. It makes you win the things you have always wanted. Since you have seen it first hand, you will be grateful for what you are able to achieve.

This is a sign that the universe is by your side. Supporting you. Applauding to your hardwork. Granting you more. Your big dreams are paying. All the work you have put in is returning. The interesting path you wanted to follow finally proves itself worthy of seeking and challenging. It makes you believe that every thing is possible.

You will be grateful. You won't doubt even for a minute that the world is a better place. You will be situated to give more. You won't miss the thrill and joy of life. That breeds your gratefulness. You will have a different, more interesting attitude to life. You will start to live a purposeful life. You will love all the wonders and adventures that you get in to.

You will be encouraged and equipped with amazing power that drives your life. Your life purpose will have a great place inside you. Chasing that will help you stay grounded. You will be happy because you are so much in love with what you do. You will be proud of yourself not just for what you are able to achieve, but also for what you are able to contribute.

You will be a believer. It is inevitable that you get rid of the doubt you have. You will see the potential people have. You will unlock the hidden and amazing power that lies in you. You will start to wonder how much you are able to achieve. You will start to notice your belief grow one by one. You will believe in yourself. You will believe in others.

This brings amazing change to your life - a change that is never going to stop - a change that will take you to a place you have always wanted. A place where you unlock the abundant gifts life is going to give you. You will see the belief in yourself rewarding you.

You will be free. Because you are happy pursuing your dreams, you will have inner freedom. The freedom you get will be contagious and you will be able to share it with others. This propels you to other adventures and challenges, larger and bigger things. You will see that there is no limit to what you are able to achieve. More doors will be opened in your life.

The inner peace you get opens new horizons. You will wake up every morning invigorated and happy. You will fall in love with chasing your passion and what it has to offer. You start to see the big picture and how it is able to change yourself and others. You will be thankful to the amazing life that is unfolding before you. And you will see every opportunities multiplying themselves.

This is the right attitude toward money.

There is one song I always find funny when I hear it. It says, '*They say money can't buy happiness. May be so, but it can buy me a boat.*' We understand that money alone can't buy happiness, But we know that we can't live without it. In fact Richard Koch in his famous book *'Living the 80/20 way'* says *'Money can make you happy, if you are poor'*. It is therefore no surprise that we pursue money for all our needs and that met needs usually mean happiness. Money therefore is an important aspect of our life. We make plans with our money. All sorts of plans. From personal fiancees to retirement plans, from starting a bushiness to scaling it up, from insurances to savings. No a man or a woman can live their lives without money.

But one thing is true. Money is not scarce. It is abundant, if you know how to create it and make it. Financially literate people know this fact. That is why the riches are getting richer. As Donald Walsh explained in his book *'Conversation with God.'*, money actually grows on trees. The secret to money making have been taught, written, and explained. But there is still a lot more to understand about money. Because when we see lots of people, they tend to not understand money and the making of it. But I say, just dare to work harder and smarter and money follows.

Work harder and smarter. There are always simpler ways of doing things. Money is no different. We can make money by building simple and better businesses. Mastering financial intelligence and in fact mastering money making is therefore something we can't afford to ignore. Reading different books about leadership and business and talking to people who succeeded in their business, this is the lesson you draw. It will help you master your work and industry.

All the business magnets we know today, Bill Gates, Warren Buffet and Mark Zuckerberg, to name a few, work harder and smarter. That is how their wealth is created. Master different techniques from successful people. Always learn about the industry you are in. There is no way that businesses might not succeed if they are done with a well tought planning and execution.

Thirift always works. Bruce Pasecki, writer of the book *'Do more with less.'* explains the source of the wealth of the United States. He suggests that thrift played a great role in all the developments and civilizations the country has enjoyed. And he states that all the economic power that is now the envy of every country in the world is based on the lesson of thrift that Benjamin Franklin has taught.

Have a winning attitude toward money. A winning attitude toward money is gained through financial intelligence. Weather you are employed or self employed, you own a small or a large business, you need to have a winning attitude toward money. A winning attitude toward money means mastering money and how it works. Plan your money forward. Don't put your money where it shouldn't go.

A well thought out plan will save you a big amount of money. Use financial planners to use your money wisely. Understand well where your money must go and must not go. If you are an employee, have a financial planner app and use it regularly. If you are running your own business, plan your budget, expenses and income well. Involve your people in doing so.

Don't think money is in short supply. Things seem scarce, until you find that there is only too much of them. Things seem limited, until you are flooded with a lot of them. Things seem rare, until you find that they are abundant. Money is the same. It comes abundant to those who think it is abundant and it comes scarce to those who think it is scarce. Don't limit yourself with little ideas Rather broaden your mind and explore how capable you can be.

Walk the talk. How to create your very first business?

You have a passion for something. That is true for all of us. And it seems true that some succeed in pursuing their passion while others don't. Some people who pursue their passion are those who create a business around it. They are able to turn their idea in to a reality. What sets these people apart from the others? What actually made them succeed?

It is usually difficult to tell but those who act up on their idea are better entrepreneurs. They always seem ready to do whatever it takes. Each and every effort they put in to their work takes them closer and closer to what they want to achieve. One success builds on the other and they are instantly found where they want to be. So, how do we start?

Ask yourself, *'What is holding me back?'* This is the first thing you should ask and have a good understanding about. You have one thing you always wanted to do in life and it seems impossible. It even looks like you forgot about it or you abandoned it. This usually occurs because you failed to ask yourself what is holding you back.

Answering this question helps you to bring out your passion. It makes you realize how exciting it could be to pursue your passion. It opens doors for you to think how amazing it could be doing it. It makes it easier to approach it nicely and the way you haven't ever done before. It answers the many doubts you have on yourself.

Dream and dream about it. How would it feel like to be the leader of your dream company? How would it feel like to serve customers who believe in you and your company? How would it feel like to see your business impacting people's lives? Have this kind of obsession built around your business idea. You will see how closer this is able to take you to what you want.

Build the blueprint of your future company in your mind. What you conceived in your mind, that is what you are going to make a reality. Have a great vision that will lead you to your destiny. Form your company's image in your mind from the very beginning. Walk that step that is required to move you steps forward to your dream.

Believe in it and yourself. If dream gives you the soul of your business, belief will embody it. It gives you the courage to start your business today. Since you have cleared out doubts, the belief you have on yourself and your company comes naturally. It won't be far since you reap the benefits. Your belief will take you further to the place you have dreamed for yourself.

Clear out the fear that limited you and held you back. Give your vision the power it deserves. The power that is going to shake your long held crippling thoughts. The power that is going to win over bad attitudes and deeds. The power that gives you only triumph and victory.

Given the ingredients and the recipe, a delicious food is guaranteed. This is a formula for success.

If you ask all people of the world what they want and pursue in their life, there is only one answer. It is success. Albert Enstien once said *'Character is more important than success'*. For me this seem to be a bit of a misconception. Yes, character is very important for an individual. It may earn you respect. It may earn you happiness and contentment. You may end up confident and self-aware. But all this virtues you have must mean one thing. They must mean success. Otherwise, it would mean you earned nothing.

Let me elaborate on this. What is success really? People have different definition and meaning for success. Some may call their wealth a success. Others may call their wisdom a success. Yet others may call their status a success. For me, success mean one thing. Getting what you want. If you are doing what you want to do, if you are where you want to be, if you get what you want, you are successful.

Looking at Enstien's claim from this perspective, it would be wrong to accept character as more important than success. But rather it would be more helpful and correct to state that character is just a means to an end, which is success. You build your character only to get what you want and be successful. Character alone won't mean anything. That is why every one of us in this world are after success.

So how can we be successful? Given the ingredients and the recipe, a delicious food is guaranteed. There is actually a universal formula for success. I will discuss its main components and building blocks of the formula here. The building blocks are variables where you can run and experiment with different values. The five building blocks or variables are Strong Zeal, Great Ambition, Amazing Endurance, Crazy Belief, and Exciting Passion.

Strong zeal. *'If you say you can or you can't, you are right.'* That is Henry Ford. This means, great things are easy to achieve or hard to achieve. It depends on your zeal. People with strong zeal can achieve any thing they want. Most innovations we take for granted today were once just a nightmare. A lot of discoveries we admire today were once considered impossible. The people responsible for these had the strongest zeal for what they do.

The people who want to love and nurture the zeal they have inside them are the people who will achieve the most extraordinary things the world has ever witnessed. Those who carry their zeal with them throughout their lives are those who get and enjoy all the successes the world can give. Don't give up on what you love and not so easily. Because it's only this, which will take you the furthest.

Great Ambition. People with strong zeal always instantly create great ambition for them. They usually get obsessed with their environment and the things around them. They always think how to make things better. Their innovative and creative mind gives them important problems and they usually come up with great solutions. They are usually well accustomed to addressing bigger and harder problems the world need a solution to so badly.

This will always give them a great ambition to find their purpose in life. They are wired with the dive and stamina to pursue and follow along with their dreams. The strong foundation that their purpose is built on gives them very far reaching influence and impact. Their contribution serve not just their community, but the planet. Their contagious drive for what they want to achieve in the world multiplies the impact they will bring to the lives of many.

Amazing Endurance. The purpose you pursue in life can't be achieved unless you are able to endure what life throws at you. The problems you have to overcome are a lot. We love an overnight success. Yes, it is possible. But what seems an overnight success is the result of years of ups and downs. You have to keep the passion you have with you and endure until you achieve what you want.

It is no surprise that you will come across lots of difficulties and failures. But you shouldn't be weak to give up and quit. Rather you have to learn from all your mistakes and endure until you find it. Be quick to learn from your mistakes. Try to experiment. Be brave to carry on doing what you believe in. The rest will take care of itself.

Crazy Belief. It is easy to do what you are told. It is normal to do what you found out. But it is usually crazy to do what hasn't been done. People with the craziest belief are those who achieve the most. The changes they are able to bring to the world are tremendous. The craziest beliefs of Thomas Edison, the Wright Brothers and lots of other great achievers have proved amazing innovation and success.

You may fall in the trap of doing the things you used to do over and over again. That won't bring any change to your work. You will only be able to achieve the great thing you want in the world if you always get out of your comfort zone and think differently. The most innovative things you enjoy today are the result of the craziest beliefs and thoughts of the greatest and successful people the world has seen.

Exciting Passion. Are you excited with what you are doing? Think again if you are not. Because, no a man or a woman has ever achieved success, or any thing worthy for that matter, without the exciting passion they have inside. Do you want to carry on and follow along with what you are doing? Do you want to move to unchartered territories and discover more? Do you want to see how far your capabilities and creativity are able to stretch? Don't ever give up on your passion.

Success is not reaching from one place to another with an ultrasonic jet. In fact, it is more like climbing the Himalayas. It is hard, but it should be exciting. It is difficult, but it should be rewarding. It is scary, but it should be fun. Passion is what makes sure it stays this way. You have to love the process than reaching the highest point. Dare and have fun. The rest is history.

How to turn your company in to an empire?

You might think that small companies are different from large ones. They are not. They might be different in the amount of money or the number of employees they manage. But a company is a company. You should carry the zeal and drive you have as a small company to your future empire. The need for a proper strategy and leadership as you scale up might come a challenge though. I'll share five tips on how you will be able to do it easily.

Do it like a pro. Many aspiring Entrepreneurs fall in to the trap of sweating the small stuff when they think about starting a business. The funding, staffing, marketing, sales ... etc. They think that wearing all these huts wears them off. This brings them exhaustion even before they walk the first step. Being deliberate about your actions is key to get rid of this problem. You have to do it like a pro from the beginning. Give a thorough thought to your business idea. Record every thing that comes to your mind on paper.

You also need to have a clear vision. Don't be timid about dreaming big. The vision of your company sets the personality and scope of your company. Do it bravely, creatively and honestly. You need to then put up a plan for its execution. Look for a competent co-founder. Hire an accountant and a legal adviser. Deal with the promotion and marketing tasks with professionals.

Be careful of who you hire. The people you hire determine the success or failure of your business. Look for the best people you can find for the job. Don't think that the best talents are always expensive. Experienced professionals may come unaffordable to you. But you will find competent people for a decent paycheck.

You might also make the mistake of hiring only people who are like you. People are different and you need all kinds of them. Give a good thought to find the perfect fit for the job. You don't need too many employees as a startup. Hire only the people you need for the most important jobs.

Keep your finances in check. Money is the life blood of your company. Plan your finances well from the beginning. When projecting expenses consider the maximum. When projecting income, consider the minimum. Try to diversify the inlets of your income as possible as you can.

Prepare a nice marketing and sales plan. Identify all your overheads. List out all other possible expenses. Dedicate a descent amount for contingency. Then put a good finance system in place.

Fail fast. Learn faster. This is what makes business fun. You never know how your products or services will be perceived unless you try. If you have to fail, fail fast. But learn faster. You can always improve your products or services. It is a never-ending process. Respond to market trends and customer needs. Listen to your gut, but also satisfy your customers.

This also applies to your business practices. To come up with a robust system for your company, you have to constantly improve your practices and work culture. Make it simple and productive.

Never cease to grow. Companies scale up if they never cease to grow. Prepare short-term and long-term strategies for your company. Come up with a well detailed plan to achieve them. Involve your employees in drafting your strategies. Have brain-storming sessions in groups. Don't be greedy and restrictive about ideas. Have a thorough discussion and filter out winning ideas.

You can't make your company an over night success. You can't either make it a multi-million dollar company a week after its launch. It needs a lot of hardwork with perfect leadership. The tips I provided will give you some insight on how you might be able to achieve this. Be strong and build your dream company.

Build your company culture. Staffing for success.

Companies succeed only if they are talent hubs. Startups can grow exponentially not just because they are lucky, but also because they make themselves center of excellence. Small and Medium size companies can scale up only if they have the human power they need. Large companies can only sustain and answer the needs of their customers only if they hire smart thinkers. The fight for talent is fierce.

Companies that perfectly understand their vision are able to build a better talent pool. If they don't understand what they are looking for, the employees they hire end up being place holders. This creates a big problem for the company and drags it in to the ashes.

Talent comes in all sorts of forms, and companies need all of it. Leaders need to take care of the need for it and its balance. There are four types of employees you need in your company. *The Deliverers* that you let to your company and nurture, *The Achievers* that you invite and give executive positions, *The Impresssors* that you hunt to introduce and promote creativity, *The innovators* that you explore and give autonomy to take your company and its products forward.

The Deliverers. These are the type of employees every company needs. You have a company means you will instantly need some one to share some of your burdens. That is why you should let deliverers to your company. You delegate the tasks that need little supervision and experience to these employees.

Many companies have employees that have stayed in the company for years, that climbed up the corporate ladder and assumed the highest possible position. Sataya Nadella of Microsoft and Sundar Piachi of Google are examples for this. These types of employees are the ones that you should nurture and retain. They might end up the people who carry the future of the company on their shoulders. You should make sure they understand the company's vision perfectly.

The Achievers. Well nurtured deliverers are soon turned achievers. You might also find achievers that perfectly match your needs from prestigious companies in similar industries that have experienced people. You should invite these people to your company with a careful and well executed hiring procedure. Achievers are a good fit for managerial positions.

You as a leader should empower and give them the executive power they need. Weather your company scales up largely or not depends on these employees. If they proved to be a reliable and important employees that your company can't afford to lose, you should promote them. If they get bored and found their position less challenging, they might flee to another company. This will hurt your company greatly.

The Impressors. Who doesn't want to get impressed. Imperssors are the life of your company. You may impress with your products if you have impressive engineers, chemists, leaders ... in your company. You may impress with your service if you have impressive marketers, sales people, clerks ... in your company. You should hunt these people. They are the ones who shape and build winning system in your company.

Impressors are creative people. Creativity needs time. You should give them all of it. Creativity needs freedom. You should give them all of it. Take a good care of them. But don't easily give up or surrender. How creative can they get? - more creative than they can. So demand creativity from impressors. Companies with the best impresssors are winners in the market.

The Innovators. Market saturation for products is not the same as it used to be. Even the most incredible and disruptive products fade to be relevant within a year or two. Only innovative companies can overcome the competition. If you don't give innovation the attention it deserves, your company won't even be able to keep afloat. Innovators make sure that this doesn't happen. You should explore and assess the talent market for these very important people. They should experiment with the science, technology, industry and market trends. They should also deliver faster and timely. They should then adjust and repeat.

Innovators should be given autonomy. Don't interfere too much on their job. Have periodical discussions and brainstorming sessions with them. These are the people who determine the quality and worth of your future products. Celebrate these people since they take your industry forward.

Understand your employees and their talent well. Getting out their talent and all what they can offer should be your task as a leader. Balance all types of employees you hire for maximum achievement.

Chapter Two - We are in a business of selling. The customer dynamics.

If there is one important thing you have to understand in business, it is your customers. Understanding your customers will help you reach your goals. The direction and fate of the company is totally based on your understanding of customers. The plans you put forth - strategic plans, short term plans, business development plans, sales plans, marketing plans all of these succeed if you understand your customers well.

Satisfying customers needs is therefore the main task of a company. Besides doing researches and surveys, the company should deliver products and services that speak to customers. Besides running amazing advertisements on media, the company should deliver competent customer services. This chapter is about understanding the customer dynamics, therefore.

Put all your intuition and smart on what you do. It's sure that you'll take the market by storm.

Do your customers relate to your business easily? Have they established connection with your business? If you answered yes, you are lucky. If you answered no, then this is what you should focus on. Businesses in which customers establish relationship with are always successful. Customers feel safe, respected and well served.

To build a business of this kind, you have to put all your intuition on what you do. You will be loved by customers who find your business interesting. You will also be able to win the market. If you follow your intuition, you can put emotion on your customers. That is why you find customers who treat your company as their choice and consider themselves a family.

Your intuition defines your business. Your company stands unique because of your uniqueness. This uniqueness will enable you to define your business. And this is possible when you put your intuition at work. As your business personally means everything to you, your customers are going to be touched by the contagious nature of your passion.

You will gather the best talent in your company and they too will love your company. Lots of people will look up to your company. Your company stands exemplary to other companies. You will start to wonder and be surprised by how much you will be able to accomplish.

Your intuition drives your business. If you follow your intuition you will see that you have a strong derive that push your business forward. Your intuition determine the culture of your company and it will be unstoppable. It will serve you as a source of discipline and determination. It will come up as the trusted source of drive and motivation.

Your intuition determine your success. '*Our product was amazing and we were successful because we built it for ourselves.*' This is Steven jobs when talking about the success of iPod and iTunes. Following your intuition and putting your smart is a determinantal factor for your company's success. You won't find another reliable friend to turn to. It guarantees your success.

Since you are talking to your customers directly with your products, it is no surprise that your company succeeds. Customers find it lovable and adorable. The emotional connection they have with your business makes them long standing customers. And every time you come up with new products or services, you are going to take the market by storm.

Your intuition helps you thrive. Your intuition will also serve you to build success after success. Growth will definitely happen because you seize every opportunity for your company's growth. And your intuition is going to help you with this too because it forms your vision. You will finally be able to make your company irresistible.

Master the art of negotiation. It all strats with selling what you have.

Yes, I said selling. You listened me saying money grows on trees. How else would you think this happens without selling. And how else would you sell without a good negotiation skill. People think selling is overwhelming. It is, if you don't know the art of negotiation. And the reason why people hate to sell is because they hate to negotiate. Mastering the art of negotiation is a necessary skill to master as an entrepreneur, therefore.

There are different out comes to every negotiation. You are an ideal sales man means you almost come a winner out of almost every negotiation. That is what turns in to your company's capital. How do you come out closing the deals from the negotiations you make? The secret always lies in one thing. In selling what you have. People hate fake sales men and women. People like sales men and women who sell honestly.

It is common to make claims that make your products and services stand out. You flaunt interesting features, guarantee quality and promise affordable price. But if the features you flaunted, or the qualities you guaranteed, or the price you promised are fake, people are not going to buy you. And even if they buy you the first time, they are not going to buy you the next time. It is therefore important and necessary to sell what you have, and sell it honestly and nicely. So, how do you sell what you have with a good negotiation skill?

Don't think what you sell is useless. Let me tell you a good news. If you think you have some thing you can sell, you usually have an incredible thing to sell. Business is usually formed with idea that came interesting to one aspiring entrepreneur and though most people find it difficult to accept the first time, its awesomeness won and it prevailed over time.

Your idea may also be some thing that your community is very much accustomed to. You should consider this an opportunity than some thing to be afraid of. Even your product may be some thing you consider a luxury. That is not going to be a problem either.

Don't make the mistake of thinking your business a failure because your customers found your products new and difficult to accept the first time. In fact, what wins customers hearts is the nobleness of your product. So, this must add to the belief you have in your idea, not to the reasons to quit it.

Don't think what you sell is less. If you believe in your idea, your customers are going to do the same. Customers don't mind the price they pay for amazing products and services. Therefore don't think that customers aren't going to pay what they are asked because they will get the price costly.

Don't underestimate the power of your idea and the passion you have for it. Your great products and services deserve your great customers. It is this zeal you have that fuels it and make it a successful business. Have trust on your idea and have trust on the products and services you built around it. You will make a number of customers that trust you.

What makes an idea sell, what makes a business a success is the purpose it serves. Don't underestimate what your aspirations are able to bring. Don't undervalue how far your passion is able to take you. Any thing that we see today sell for higher price is the result of a purposeful idea.

Don't think what you sell is not needed. Okay, you believe in your idea and you know it is great. But you might doubt if you are going to find customers that are going to pay your bills. What guarantees loyal customers to a business is amazing products and services built around amazing ideas.

Amazing ideas, if executed well are are going to win the hearts of many customers. They will be paying any price they are asked and they will be paying willingly. You will win over a number of customers since your product is going to win the market.

Because customers are going to love your business, your business is going to sustain. Customers are going to need your products and services eagerly. You will be able to get customers who might even worship your business.

Don't think what you sell is not important. Your business is great because it adds value to people's lives. It is necessary to pursue your idea and tap its full potential, therefore. The thrill of what you do is the passion you have for your business and the power of your business to change people's lives.

This will help you to continue to do it as a business. The problems it solve and the benefits it offer will make it needed more and more. The satisfaction you give your customers and the respect customers give you in each and every possible encounters will make your business grow.

Don't ever doubt that your business is not going to succeed. Given your dedication and commitment, and your excellent and outstanding service, your business is not only going to succeed, but also propel. You made your business the most important thing in the world and it will prove itself the most important business.

Think what you sell is amazing. You will instantly see your business serving your goal. You will believe that what you sell is amazing and incredible. What else would you want other than meeting your goal? In fact, what else would you want other than a business built around your goal?

That is why you wouldn't be working even a single day of your life since you are doing what you want to do. You will say to yourself *'This is what I want to do for the rest of my life.*' It will mark the beginning of life as you have never imagined it before.

You will see your passion grow each and every day. The idea that was once just a thought grows in to an amazing and big business that thrills you. And the business you built will not fail to impress you, not even just for a moment.

Unpredictability gives customers the surprise and thrill they deserve. Hold on to it.

Customers love surprises. When they are provided with solutions they have been dreaming about, they will be thrilled. They love the company which serve them with this kind of products and services. Companies which are unpredictable are the ones which are able to provide this. And this will be in the company's DNA if it values and runs on innovation.

There may be different approaches to make a company unpredictable. The way the company is run, the culture the company has, the way it responds to customers' concerns and how well and nicely it reaches customers determine the company's unpredictability. Companies which run answering these are the ones who will succeed to make customers fall in love with them.

They did it. Unpredictable companies are the envy of other companies. Not just the companies which are in the same industry but also companies which are in other industries. They are examples in what it requires to achieve the impossible. They show leading the way every now and then. They are exemplary in how they lead innovation and creativity.

They approach a problem differently. They know they are able to deliver a solution. Therefore, they employ different tactics to achieve it. It always turns out that what they do pays. They are also smart in how they make decisions. This prevents them from a deadlock. Customers love these companies because they never fail to impress them.

This is how we do things around here. These companies also have a culture of promoting amazing practices and methods. They have strong system in place. They always test and adjust their practices. They innovate not only in their products but also in the system they build in their company. They promote strong communication within their employees.

You are very welcome. In these companies, customers are treated like a family. Their voices are heard. Customers know it is their company. And the company knows how to serve them. These type of companies put a winning customer service in place. Customers are going to love it because they never feel left alone.

Isn't it amazing. Because these companies reach customers through different channels, customers are served well. They know how to promote themselves and what image their company should have in customers' minds. They never fail to fulfill their promises. Customers are never going to let down these companies, therefore.

Are you a trend setter or a trend follower? The art of differentiation.

You are in business to see the change you want to bring to the world. You know what you want to achieve. You walked some steps to achieve that. Two things might happen. Your business might get all the attention and a lot of customers may love it and adopt it very fast. It is also possible that, despite all the efforts and endeavors you made, you are no where close to what you want for your business. There is nothing pleasing than seeing your products or services being appreciated and gain traction. The products we got from Microsoft, Apple, Google and Facebook are examples to this. They succeeded in being the mainstream of Hardware, Software, Search Engine and Social Media. They set the trend of their business.

Where as companies like Netscape, Yahoo, Myspace failed to achieve what the former companies had achieved. This is not just because of the quality of the products they offered but their failure to be the trend setters. What is trend setting? It just means one thing. It is inventing the future. The products and services you create should be built experimentally and incrementally to achieve this. You have to make sure that what you offered is here to stay. What do companies need to be the trend setters then?

Be clear about what you want from your products or services. What determines the success of your business and the products and services you deliver is how well you understand your idea and how well articulated it is. Ideas can be born from any where. These ideas that come to your mind can't be multi million dollar ideas at first thought. You have to stay obsessed with them and think about them very well. Put every thing that comes to your mind on paper. Think about ways of making it better and better every day. Adjust and shape it until you are satisfied with it.

Being clear about your products and services is the first step to win over your competition and win the market. It has the potential to make your business a success even before its launch. You have to think about how you differentiate your products. Set goals for yourself and your customer that your products and services should achieve. Google achieved the number one spot in the search engines war because it offered internet users with better and relevant search results. That is because of the way the search engine is wrote and how it is programmed to work.

Understand your customers very well. It is natural to think your products from your perspective. You are after all doing this to solve the problems you saw. You have your own way of achieving this. This may bring a solution to the problem. But it won't be even close to that product your customers are going to love. That's why you have to put yourself on your customers' shoes. Try to understand your customers very well. Try to get in to their mind. Try to know how they think. That will give you the answer about what they want from your product.

Customers are never going to say no to your products and services if you give them what they want. They will be early adopters, fans and even evangelists of your business. Products that talk to customers needs and wants are always winners in the market. Don't stop to address and answer their questions. Even try to give them assignments on how they would love your future products and services look like. That will prove you the market leader position.

Experiment, adjust, test and repeat. You know what you want. You know what your customers want. You have came up with the product. And still some thing is not right. No one seems satisfied. What is wrong? One thing is missing - they way you solved your customers needs. There are lots of ways of solving the problems. Don't limit yourself with the first solution you are able to come up with. You have to experiment with your team. List and try out all the possibilities. Adjust your product and come up with demos and samples. Test them with selected customers of every target groups you might think. Repeat this process again and again.

Neat and elegant products are the result of doing this. Customers always find it very simple to know the difference your products have over the others. Help the people in your team to come up with new ways of doing things. Always think about how your product can be able to evolve. The products of apple are ideal example to this. How they evolved from the ipod to the ipad, from the apple mac to the mac book and the versions of iphone is very amazing.

Keep it simple and stupid. The best solutions are always the easiest ones. You may think of a lot of features packed in to one product. That is not a problem. You may also think to solve lots of problems. That is not a problem either. What you should think about is to make your products simple and elegant. It is possible to achieve this. List out all the things you want on your product. Try to experiment with them and put them in a structured way. You may add new ones, or you may get rid of some. Come up with simple ways of incorporating these in your product.

Don't make the user find it hard to use your product. Make it easier for them to accomplish what they want from your product. Make it usable. Follow common practices and standards. But don't forget to solve it in a different and simple way. Customers love world class products. Put all your smarts in them. You are going to be impressed with what you'll be able to achieve.

Don't stop innovating. With this capitalist market where competition is fierce and disruptive products are made available every day, innovation is the only way to stay ahead in the market. Have your talented people work on ways of improving your products and solving newer problems. Customers will never stop to love and look for your newer products. Come up with newer and newer ways of bringing newer and newer solutions.

Make your company a place of innovation and experiment where great ideas are born. You have to always take your industry and business forward. Offer excellent ways of communicating with your customers. Address the problems you see in your products constantly. Don't disappoint your customers because of your failure to listen and respond. Never fail to impress them because of your failure to innovate and experiment.

How can you grow your customer base exponentially and make your business a success?

Your business is your life and your customers keep it alive. The business idea you have, the research you make, the planning you put forth, the way you execute it - all of these should be done customers in mind. Okay so, you know what problem to solve for your customers, you understand your niche market, you decided how to get to your customers mind and do it the way you would be able to impress them. Your business is up and running. Days, weeks, months gone by and you have just won only a few customers, nowhere close to where you imagined.

You may wonder why customers are not flocking to your business. You have nice products, your shop is nice looking, you have every thing all set. So why aren't you getting more customers? People love businesses for different reasons. They may love a business for the quality of the product. They may love a business for its fair price. They may love a business for its reliability. They may love a business for its brand. They may love a business for its eloquence and style. For what ever reason customers might love your business, you should be able to have a number of them and build your business quick enough. How can you grow your customer base exponentially and make your business a success?

Cold calling works. Cold calling exists for a reason. In fact the phone directory at your table or from a well-known website has a lot of power on it. Its value starts not when you start cold calling. Its worth is from the time you thought about starting a business and you started researching. It helps you identify your target customers and be clear about your niche market. It might even enable you get potential customers before your business kicks in. You have to start to prepare your customers base which includes potential companies that you think will readily accept your products or services. You will be better off using CRM software that you might be able to find for free or a couple of bugs online.

Cold calling may seem satisfying at first when you talk to two or three companies that respond well. But after you made some more calls, you will soon understand how frustrating it is. You will find companies that will treat you badly. Your confidence starts to slip and you will lose the courage to continue. The next time you intend to make another one, you will be afraid how the other end is going to receive you. This pattern continues until fear keeps you away from doing any more calls. You have to check this behavior before it happens.

One way of getting around this is to prepare ice breaking speeches and other phrases that might help you easily communicate. You will instantly see a pattern emerging. Identify common scenarios and be prepared to come up with interesting and short questions and answers. These especially will help you if you have a telemarketing software. Talking to customers will instantly come second nature to you. Another way you might be able to ease your frustration is by recording your followup calls. You may record the voice or write a summary of the call. This will save you time and makes your communication precise the next time you make a call.

Don't make the mistake of chasing difficult and uncooperative customers. They will drain your energy and time. Decide when you are going to stop chasing a lead. Otherwise, you may lag behind your sales target and the company will loose loads of money. Develop better communication skills. Have fun getting to know different types of people. Results are going to accrue.

Referrals work better. Customers you cold call are complete strangers. You may need a number of followups to get to know them and others more to close a deal. The process is a bit lengthy and costly. Using referrals makes the process easier and less awkward. If you are able to get leads that you found interesting but not able to turn into customers, ask them nicely if they know any other business that might find your product or service beneficial. If you are able to close deals with customers, take your time and try to know the nature of their business well. Try to extract as much information as you can about their industry and don't be shy to ask them to suggest you as many referrals as they can.

Use different tools when you reach out for referrals. You may use surveys or questioners. You may also request recommendation letters and testimonials from your best customers. This will help you get to know your niche market very well and it extends and make your customer base richer.

Relationship marketing works best. Two of the methods we just discussed are a bit traditional and come a bit challenging. Although you will be able to secure a considerable amount of customers from these endeavors, their potential to turn leads into customers is limited. It also lacks the potential to retain customers longer. Relationship marketing is a perfect choice to get your customers and make them stay longer. You will be able to find most of your best customers using this approach. You may find these customers from your cold calling and referrals. You may also find them from your support system.

Try to satisfy the needs of these customers better. Don't hesitate to help them with all your power. Take time to understand their company and their industry. Involve them in your company meetings and discussions about your future products and services. These are the customers you wouldn't want to miss. They turn your mission into a reality and your company a success.

Brand can't be out of the equetion. So you have a business idea. You got a blue print for its execution. You know the expertise and effort it's going to need. How are you going to make yourself inspired and stay motivated by your business all the way through to the end? And how are customers going to ask themselves if they could be able to be fine without your business? That is brand. And you can't make it out of the equation.

If you think you have a good sense of art, try to put all your wish for your business on the name, logo, interior and exterior design, paper and digital promotional and corporate identity materials. Don't forget to talk to a professional designer though. I tell you. It won't be long till your customers start to relate to your business. They will soon turn a family.

Love your brand and work for it. Never stop to give it the attention it deserves. Your brand should tell your company's story. Always align it with your mission and the culture you want to build in your company. Customers respond to brand. Don't disappoint them. But rather impress them day in and day out with unpredictability and style. Customers are going to notice and grow in number in a short period of time.

Smart marketing and sales force make it all happen. And what about the team who makes all this happen? Be very deliberate about the marketing and sales team you build. Have a good marketing and sales plan. Be creative about how the team executes it. Supervise them closely so you don't miss the thrill of achieving your projected sales. A good sales team is able to give your company the loyal and satisfied customers it needs.

How you build and see your company defines your customers. How customers respond and react defines your business. Take a good care of your business while building your customer base. Take a good care of your customers while building your business. That is how you are going to be able to win the market and achieve the success you deserve.

Influencing customers' decisions.

I am always interested in one thing in my business. Closing deals. It's amazing how it comes so simple at times and how it comes the hardest thing other times. You love customers who understand your business, adore your passion of solving their problems, pay happily for your service, and support your mission to give them more. You won't ever lose the drive you need to run and grow your business.

There are also difficult customers. You listen them, you do what they want, you surprise them, you support them with all your expertise and what will you finally get? Rejection. It is the hardest thing in the world to understand these customers. It's not that you fail to close the deal or win their heart. It is that you can't get to connect to them in any way possible. It is the rejection that hurts you too much and leave you disappointed.

This all boils down to one thing. Decision making. The way we make decision determines the success or failure of our business. We humans don't like to be told what to do. We want to decide for ourselves. We love to make decisions that we don't regret. We want to make decisions we love. Every actions we take, every things we buy, every choices we make, every things we do, they all need our decision. And the decisions we make determine what we get, weather we succeed or not. We don't want to feel used and played. We don't want to get lost and disappointed. So how do we make decisions any way?

People usually make decision when it feels right. It is very complex how they decide, but there is always a point where they say *'I damn love this.'*, or *'Sure, I'll take it.'* or *'Okay, It'll be fine.'*. You can make decisions in two ways. Voluntarily or Involuntarily. Voluntary decisions are made by considering risks and opportunities, pros and cons, benefits and drawbacks. They involve lots of deliberation. Where as involuntary decisions are made by intuition and gut feeling. You just decide.

You usually make involuntary decision for the things you are well aware of. Your intuition is well developed and you can usually decide easily. But when you have little know how about what to do, you always need to make voluntary decision. You have to ask yourself about what you need and you'll be able to develop better understanding of your likes and preferences. Both voluntary and involuntary decisions are important. We should be using both of them.

If involuntary decision comes naturally to you, then you most possibly have an inclination toward it. You must try to understand and nurture your interest. You will be needing to study and try to perform better. You'll be needing to make voluntary decision, therefore. If you usually make voluntary decisions, that usually mean you have wider variety of interests and better understanding at lots of things. You'll instantly be skilled and talented in lots of things and be able to make involuntary decisions. Let's look at the main things that make up our decision making.

Involuntary decision (Avoiding wrong doing)

Mistake When you make involuntary decision, the first thing you usually do is to avoid mistake. You consider if you get what you want with the price you are willing to pay. You avoid buying the things you don't want. You avoid paying more than you want.

Regret No one wants to regret the decisions they made. Especially about the things they buy. They therefore avoid regret. If you made too many mistakes in your buying decision, you'll most definitively regret. Or if you gave up some thing you wanted badly, regret is a sure thing to happen.

Voluntary Decision (Avoiding inadequacy)

Negligence. As voluntary decision involves deliberation, buyers usually avoid negligence. You closely look at errors and any faults in what you buy. You test what you want to buy from different aspects and points.

Conformity. Standards and conformity mean different things for different people. Fashion and trend is a question of conformity. If you say you conform or you don't, that is what speaks to you. But when you decide voluntarily, you try to avoid failure of the things you consider valuable in the things you buy.

It is therefore a good practice to know customers preferences and notice how they make their decision. It increases the likely hood of your persuasion and the satisfaction of the customer that buys it.

How can you win fierce competition? Standing out from the crowd.

One of the challenges that you face as a new and growing company is the fierce competition you will face. It may come very hard to win the market. What will enable you to win over the competition is to stand out from the crowd. You have to impress customers with the uniqueness and likability of your business. You have to come as a business where customers find intriguing.

One of the things you might do is to study your industry very well. You have to understand how things work. You may need to do different assessments. And you may need to develop different skills. You may learn from other businesses and people. Then you have to come up with strategies and methods of your own to win the market.

Who do you sell to. The first thing you have to do is to differentiate your customers. To understand this, you have to study your competitors. Your business should be unique and different. The solution you provide must be one that is not addressed by other competitors. And one thing that shows the uniqueness of your business is the customers you sell to.

You must refine your business idea following your understanding of the customers you want to serve. You may find it difficult to identify the uniqueness of your business at first. It doesn't always and totally need to be different from your competitors. Just think about different ways of solving a problem. Make it appeal for different type of customers and try to challenge the status quo.

How do you sell it. Now that you know how to differentiate your market, you have to know how you sell it to customers. You need to be creative in how you make sales in your company. You have to develop your sales skills. You may hire sales people too. Prepare marketing and sales plans. Brainstorm on strategies and actions needed to achieve it.

Empower yourself and your sales team. Invent different ways of fulfilling customers needs. Learn as much as you can about what your customers want. Solve their problems. Impress your customers with your care and understanding.

Now you know the market. Your marketing endeavors will pay and you will start to notice changes in your sales. This means you now have some understanding about your customers. Build on this. This will show you the direction your company should be going. And it will enable you understand your company very well.

Focus on innovation. Your understanding of your company will enable you to form strategies. And following these strategies, new business frontiers will open. Study the moves you should be taking and do it without losing focus. Don't just focus on profit maximization rather make your company emerge as an innovative and creative one.

People are happy when they get amazing products and services. What is in a brand actually?

All of us have a brand that we relate to the most. We choose that brand because it speaks to us. We love it from our heart that we pay any thing we are asked to make it our own. We even become an evangelist for it. We want to even be referred as *'the guy or the girl that loves ...'*. This is what brand is. It is the appreciation we have for quality. It is the respect we have for awesomeness. It is the choice of our life style.

Brand makes people trust a company. Brand makes a company reliable. And most of all, brand makes customers happy. It is not easy to win the title of *'The most trusted company'* or *'The most reliable company'* or *'The most loved company'*. You need to earn it. It is a reward you get from your customers. It is a testimony for your amazing work. So, what is in a brand actually?

Your company's principle is in a brand. Nike, the world largest producer of foot ware and apparels, is an example as to how a company's principle is what makes up a brand. Because of the company's effort to make itself a choice for amazing foot ware, it is able to win the market. Nike is related to winning. All the amazing stars of sports have wore its products.

The company's principle is based on celebrating sports and greatness. It supports different sporting events. It is in sporting researches. It offers different health products. The company's brand is well accepted that it became a sign of health and awesomeness. It is wore by not just great athletes but different celebrities in entertainment, fashion and tech.

Your company's values are in a brand. Apple is an example in how a company's values translates in to an amazing brand. The company has always made art the center of its innovation and creativity. It has always been after products that perfectly show the intersection between art and tech. Because the company's values revolve around this, it has emerged as the producer of the world's finest tech products.

It is impossible not to see apple's products and imagine what the company's values are. Customers are fascinated by apple's products because it is lovable. Apple's love of art is not just in its outlook, but also in the design and architecture of the product. It has been built with care and creativity that it makes it the world finest tech product. And the company stands as an example of a great brand.

Your company's story is in a brand. '*Ask not what your country do to you. Ask Coca Cola*'. That was CNN mocking Donald Trump. Coca cola is the single most loved soft drink in the world. If you ask people for the world most loved brands, I am sure that coca cola tops the list. Coca cola is an amazing brand because it tells stories. The situations that makes coca cola relevant are so many.

It is hard not to think coca cola where there is recreation. Coca cola even tries to relate to you on a personal level. When your brand tells amazing stories, it is easy to be accepted and adored. Because we easily relate to stories, your brand should tell one.

What you should do to make the market work for you rather than against you?

You have a product. You have solved something which was left unaddressed. The next thing you should do is to market your product. To make the market work for you, you need to have excellent marketing strategy. Other wise the market will stand against you without you even noticing. What should our marketing endeavors look like to sustainably win the market then?

One single most beneficial thing you can do is to make your business customers centered. You have to understand that working for the market means working for your customers. That was your passion. Solving something. Now that you have solved it, you have to communicate well with your customers. A business not well communicated is a business lost.

Win customers' hearts. Step on to your customers shoe. Know their likes and dislikes. When you have touched their button, you will see the market responding. You have made promises and when you keep them and in fact, when you do it with a surprise, you will win your customers' hearts. Make your marketing campaigns speak to your customers.

Your product may come with different features. You believe that it is helpful. But if you fail to market them well, you will be losing your company. What are the benefits of your product? List them out. Build up success stories with customers. Study how uniquely your products are solving customers needs. Give customers more and more reasons why they should buy your product.

Reach your customers often. Once you win customers, don't let your relation with them be broken. Make them families to your company. Reach them frequently. Earn their loyalty. Use their testimony to reach to other customers. Build the confidence they have on you. Have discussion with them about how better you can serve them. Shape your company's future with them.

Don't see the money you spend on understanding your customers a loss. You actually need to take some care with your spending on marketing. If you do it perfectly, it is going to pay back. When you make your marketing moves, do your experiments. You will find out better ways of serving your customers. You will come up with better ways of winning the market.

Earn customers' trust. Never fail to hear your customers' voices. Listen to what they say and make it your business's agenda. You will end up building their trust. This will have a multiplier effect. You will notice your customer base grow. This give you the courage to go the extra mile - to always fulfill customers' needs - to always fill in the gap - to always serve customers better.

Chapter Three - Habits and practices for you and your company that lead to fruition. - Self Development.

Your company needs its own persona. It has its own ways of doing things, solving problems, and collaborating one another. This forms your company culture which is the reflection of the habits and practices in your company. You should take time to see and note its effect, therefore. You should test and measure the habits that drive your company. You should adjust and improve the practices that lead your company.

And this includes you and your employees. The company should value self development. The changes you and your employees make personally makes a lot of difference. It helps your company to stay strong and competitive. It also makes your company's goals met and your efforts lead to fruition. You have to be careful and selective as well as creative and inventive in the habits and practices you set in your company.

Dare to make your own destiny. How self-made entrepreneurs use their imagin-ation to find their purpose in life.

Life is amazing. There are lots of wonders it offers. Life is fantastic. There is so much fun it gives. Life is fulfilling. There is plenty to share and be happy. Don't take it for granted. Use your imagination to achieve your goals. Build your strength. Use your smart to make the game wonderful. This makes you the determined and diligent person you are now. This is you.

And follows your purpose. You are living your life in its full grace. Nothing can hold you back, because your purpose has the power to overcome your obstacles, no matter how big they seem. Nothing can stop you because what you do is amazing. The purpose you have in this world awaits you to make your life awesome. You may not notice it but having a purpose in life makes all the difference.

Love your life. Put a little ambition to it. It carries you throughout your life. It carries you to a place where you have never dreamed. Stay motivated. It gives your life a thrill. Stay inspired. It makes your life delightful. Stay curious. Life has a lot to give. Be interested in chasing meaning in your life. Because it will help you get originality in it.

Dream big. You will see it is possible. The problem that once seemed unavoidable vanishes. The place that once seemed unreachable will be conquered. You will go from success to success. You will triumph over your hardships. You will find yourself serving your vision. You will see it take shape. Your big dream moves you to the unbeatable domain.

You will find your true calling. Nothing feels wrong. Rather every thing feels right. It feels perfect actually. Now that you understand your calling, nothing holds you back. You will discover your best self. Your will start to live your life the way you have never lived it before. Your purposeful life will start to change everyday. Passion and zeal will characterize your life. You will meet your true calling and your calling will meet you.

You see meaning in everything. Life gives you its pleasantness. You shouldn't go far to see and witness that life is so amazing. You will find it by your side. Where ever you go, whatever situation you are in, happiness is with you. Because your peace comes out from the inside, you will have it not just for yourself but, you will have a lot to share. Life rewards you because you cared. You are led to the destiny you have made for yourself.

Pursue your dreams and make it big. The road to achieving it is what makes it interesting.

'*As long as you are dreaming, make it big.*' says Donald Trump. Big dreamers are able to achieve great goals. They are able to change the world. Set great goals for yourself that drives you. Pursue it until you make it a reality. It won't be easy, but it will be amazing. It won't be simple, but it will be fascinating. The road that you follow is full of adventures and thrills. It is interesting and worth following.

All great men and women have been there. They have seen how big dreams make up life's purpose. They have seen how it is wonderful to pursue them. They have witnessed the change they are able to make to our world. Their work therefore stands as an undying testimony of the power of dreaming big. What are big dreams actually made of? What do they constitute?

Great goal. It speaks to you. It makes your heart full of excitement. It takes control of you and take you to the wonder planet. You have this amazing feeling when you talk about it. You have this amazing fun doing it. You have this amazing happiness seeing it work. That is your goal. That is what your dream is made of; the great goal you are pursuing.

It gives your life a purpose. It shows you the wonders in life. It makes you fall in love with life. Pursuing it is an excitement. Being obsessed with it is a bliss. Looking at its fruition is a delight. You have no hesitation, but follow it. You have no reservation, but do it. You have no doubt, but enjoy it. That is your goal. That is what your dream is made of; the great goal you are pursuing.

Strong enthusiasm. It took control of you. You breath it. It puts hunger in you. You do it more often. It fills you with excitement. You enjoy it. There is nothing like it that you wanted so badly. There is nothing like it that you pursued this far. There is nothing like it you searched with eagerness. This is your enthusiasm. It is what your dream is made of; the strong enthusiasm you have for your goal.

You have all the interest to accomplish it. You have the strongest determination to achieve it. You have the mental resolve to attain it. This is your enthusiasm. It is what your dream is made of; the strong enthusiasm you have for your goal.

Bold heart. You have never been this courageous to follow your dream. You have never been this daring to achieve your dream. You have never been this brave to reach your dream. This is your heart. It is what your dream is made of; the bold heart you have which takes you to your goal.

Genuine smart. You learn what ever it takes to make it happen. You pay what ever it takes to make it happen. You do what ever it takes to make it happen. This is your smart. It is what your dream is made of; the genuine smart you have that makes your goal a reality.

Dare to understand yourself better. Self-awareness takes you further.

You have your own attributes. Likes and dislikes, interests and choices, talents and gifts. Understanding yourself well helps you to be your best self. It leads you to success in all endeavors you pursue in life. Self-awareness is therefore key to achieve better and sustainable results. There are a number of ways you may take to understand yourself.

You may take personality tests. You may challenge yourself in any situations you find yourself in. Your characters are sometimes hidden. You may unlock your true nature if you dare to ask. This will lead you to greater results because you are acting toward your personality. Any thing else that is against your nature end up you being lost.

Understand your natural inclination. What are those things you find yourself inclined to. Are you in to science or sports? Do you love arts or politics? You will start to unlock your untouched potential when you understand your inclination. You will find it easier to form your life purpose and pursue it. There is a reason that you should understand your inclination.

You may not find your true calling easily. You should walk some steps to identify the things that fascinate you and start to chase them. You will find yourself excel and shine. List out the things you would love most and learn as much as you can about them. Do this again and again until you find your true calling in life.

Understand your preferences. The other thing that define your personality is your preferences. Your preferences say a lot about yourself. They are also the reflection of your values. What ever you want to achieve in your life, understanding your preferences will help you greatly. It will make sure that you are not swimming against the current.

Understand what type you are. There are may tools developed to help you understand yourself better. These tools are developed to help you what type of person you are. Although it is very hard to tell the whole story in setting some categories, it is very helpful to understand our similarities and differences. It helps you to communicate and cooperate with people better besides knowing yourself.

Understand what you are good at. Self-awareness helps you to form your life purpose. Your effort to know yourself better results in understanding what you are good at. As an entrepreneur, it gives you the courage and motivation to pursue your dreams. It helps you identify what you want to do in your life. And it greatly impacts your success.

When you are self-aware, it is easy for you to pursue your dreams. It gives you the nerve to start to act now. It also determines its success. It helps you to be the person you have always wanted to be. You will be so grateful that your wishes are fulfilled.

Our mind is capable of mastering any challenges you give it. Harness its power for amazing results.

We have our most sophisticated and mysterious organ inside our skull. The brain. It is the master of our body. It is made of billions and billions of neurons. Harnessing its power will lead you to great results. To make the most out of your mind, you have to do some exercises that help. Our mind is capable of change. The more challenges you give it, the more capable it becomes.

There are some proven ways of making our brain fit. Doing this practices most often enables our mind to be flexible. It makes it learn different things easily. As our brain is given some challenges and as it learns something new, more connections are formed between neurons. As more connections are formed between neurons, there will be fast communication and processing between all its neurons and it becomes vigorous.

This practices will bring both chemical and physical changes to our brain. Neuroplasticity enables our brain change. Apart from forming new connections, the physiology of the brain also changes. There is also change in the neurotransmitters and other chemicals that are found in our brain. To promote the creation of hormones and chemicals that are useful to our brain, as well as to make physiological changes such as a smaller amygdala and larger frontal lobe, the brain has to do some useful exercises.

Learn new skills. One of the best exercises you can give our mind is to learn new skills. You will get sharper and sharper mind. You may learn a new language or a musical instrument. You may also train your mind with skills that help your career. Or you may do some staff as a hobby that may challenge you a bit. There are also plenty of games that keep your mind fit.

There is nothing adventurous as learning a new skill. There is a learning cure you will pass though. It is fascinating at first. But after some time, you may get bored. Mastering any new skill requires repetition and practice. You have to continue practicing if you have to master that skill. It requires some patience. But after you have passed this stage, you will find yourself with the new skill that you have mastered and are proud of.

Reflect on what you have learned. There is nothing like a deep discussion that makes us happy and that is capable of rewiring our brain. To reflect on what you have learned, you may pass the book you read to a friend and have a discussion about it. Or you may bring some ideas to the table and discuss about it when you are with your friends. Look for other ways of reflecting on what you have learned.

Challenge yourself. Giving yourself challenges is another thing that will help you to make your mind sharper. Pick one challenging thing you have always wanted to master and tackle it. When you have passed that challenge, give yourself another one. Start small so that you don't exhaust yourself and quit. Build up your mind through challenges one by one.

Be resilient. It is easy to quit and say '*I tried it, but it is so hard.*' You have to stay away from this kind of attitude. Nothing worthy can be earned without patience. You have to have a growth mindset to achieve any thing. Do what is required and be resilient. You will be impressed by what your mind is capable of mastering.

Form this important habits and you will see your life change.

Our day to day actions form our habits. Our life depends so much on our habits that they determine our lifestyle and success. Stopping bad habits and nurturing the good one's is therefore important. You may have different bad habits in lots of the things you do and in the different aspects of your life. They are actually standing in your way of achieving results.

It is a hard to stop bad habits as it is difficult to form good ones. It requires practice and determination. The first step to stop bad habits is to identify them. What areas of your life needs improvement or change? What habits are holding you back? List them out and tackle them one by one. Take baby steps to every change you want to make.

Sleep habits. Sleep is important for our health and productivity. You have to take enough sleep every day to function properly and stay healthy. If you sleep too little, you will suffer different consequences. Sleep deprivation is the source of stress and different mental health problems. People with insomnia are very much likely to suffer form many health concerns.

Depending on your age, what you do and your health situation, you have to have enough sleep each and every day. Apart from setting your sleeping hours, you also need to change some unhelpful habits. You have to check your alcohol intake. Besides, you need to make your sleep hours regular that doesn't change. Stop sleeping at any time other than your sleeping hours. Don't take coffee in the afternoon. This will help you have a quality sleep every night.

Eating habits. What you eat has an impact in all aspects of your life. One thing what food you eat and when you eat them has an impact on is your will power. Eating junk food heavily reduces your will power. It also causes obesity and other health concerns. Have a good diet every day so that you will stay energetic and productive the whole day.

Morning habits. The routines you do at the morning have a lot of effect on the quality of your day. One good practice is to do a physical exercise or yoga. You may also consider meditation. Other good habit you might consider at the morning is practicing gratefulness.

Keeping a Journal might also help. Get out of bed and do some of this tasks so that you have an interesting day.

Work habits. There are also important work habits you may consider for a better and productive day. One such habit is planning, your day. You may do your planning at the end of each day or at the morning. Put the most important tasks you should be doing in your plan. Put the hardest tasks first so that you are not exhausted and bored. This will stop you from procrastinating.

Take breaks in an hour or so. Taking breaks will help you stay focused. Don't cram yourself with many tasks at once. When you do multiple tasks at once, you will be distracted and kill your time switching between them. Focus on one task and execute them one by one. Disconnect from different sites and email so that you won't receive notification. Notifications will distract you and stop you from engaging at one task. Set a regular time to check your email and other websites. Your day will be very much productive.

How assertiveness helps your company be an amazing workplace.

Employees at a workplace might be productive and outstanding. They may also be mean and arrogant. While you try to understand them while hiring and interviewing, it is so unlikely that you fully understand them. A work place might turn a competent and talented employee in to a manipulative and difficult one. On the other hand, it might turn an average employee in to an excellent and outstanding one.

One thing that promotes an interesting collaboration and a healthy workplace is assertiveness. Promoting assertiveness in the work place helps employees norm each other. It makes them set clear boundaries. This will make the teams you form high performers. It reduces problems and disagreements and promotes discussion and team spirit. So, how do you promote assertiveness?

Promote excellent communication. Employees in one team and in different teams may run in to conflict. This is common. How you handle conflict is what matters. If you solve it so that they understand you value communication over conflict, that will do the trick. Leaders at all levels in your company should do the same. This helps each and every employee be assertive.

In an environment where communication and discussion is not given priority, gossip takes charge. It is very hard to promote assertiveness. Rather, tension and stress builds up. Unnecessary power plays plague the company. Every one talks about the other behind his or her back. Passive aggressiveness becomes common place. Building nice communication procedures and practices is a solution to this.

Promote healthy leadership. Employees, especially those at different management positions need excellent leadership skill. Make it clear that leadership skill is what takes employees up the corporate ladder. Make different endeavors that improve the leadership skill of your employees at all levels. Measure and evaluate the performance of leaders and celebrate the high performers.

Where there is no excellent leadership, intimidation replaces it. Assertive employees are ignored and intimidators are celebrated. Because intimidation is celebrated, every one tries to turn in to an intimidator. It will be taken as a sign of strength and good management practice. Before your company turns in to the worst workplace, show concern and promote healthy leadership.

Promote talent and competence. No one denies that a company which celebrates talent and competence excels in all aspects. Your company will be the company which is known for its over achievement. When you promote talent and competence, it will have a multiplier effect. Every one focuses on developing his or her own talent.

But if you fail to do this, many negative characters start to emerge among employees. Manipulation and bullying will be the norm. This will pose problems to the company. It will be the sign and beginning of the company's downfall. That is why you should promote talent and competence to surround yourself with assertive people that enable your company take the leap.

Don't fall into procrastination. This is how to get things done.

When was that you decided to learn french? Yes. it was three years ago. And when was that you said you will finish your project? Yes. It was eight months before. Your french studies and your project are still in your mind. What is going on? You decided to do it but still it is not done. What is the problem?

Every time you remind yourself that you should start to do it today, you give yourself some excuses and you stop doing it. You have mastered not french but procrastination. Your project is not done but instead you have mastered million ways of procrastinating it.

What a pity. You started to see that there is no one to blame, but yourself. You just think how it would have been different if you acted up on your decision. You would have mastered french and impressed your friends. You would have better communicated with the people at the french company you are working with. Your project would have been completed and you would have started to make money your company hasn't ever made before.

We have every reason to stop procrastination. It has stood on our way of successes. It is stealing our diligence one by one. It is turning our dream a nightmare. Why do we procrastinate then? What can we do about it? How can we get things done rather than push them to the I-Wish-I-Have-Done list?

You procrastinate because you are lacking something. This is the easiest as well as the hardest thing that makes you procrastinate. Let's consider the example we have seen before. You decided to learn french. But you have not done that because you don't have enough money. But if you did some savings, it would very simple to do it. You would have done it the moment you decided. But you may have never asked yourself *'What am I lacking that made me procrastinate? How can I solve this?'*

You procrastinate because you lost your will power. You have always wanted to master french. In fact you don't just love the french language but you also want it badly. But you have lost the strength to start. One reason might be because you have lost your will power. You had passion for it. But you have lost it because you haven't get it done for a long time. If you fail to take it seriously and not start doing it, you will lose your passion and instantly you will lose the will power too. Act up on your passion imminently therefore.

You procrastinate because you lack discipline. This is the project that will bring a big change in your life. In fact you are so fascinated about it that you told every one you are going to do it. But time went on and on and you haven't still started it. Your friends start to make fun of you. '*Hey Peter, humanity is going to mars before you do it.*' You look back and see what actually stopped you from doing it. You see that you have never took your project seriously. You lacked the discipline that this kind of project require. Have discipline if you want to achieve anything worth.

You procrastinate because you lack organization. You are fascinated about this project. You started it. But it is taking longer because you also started to procrastinate this and that. You failed to be organized and execute the project one by one. Your project is fascinating and therefore need organization, plan and determination it deserves.

You procrastinate because you are afraid. The zeal you had for your project was initially amazing. But instead of giving yourself more reasons to pursue it, you gave yourself more reasons that you are not able to do it. You start to build blocks between yourself and your project. This blocks got ticker and ticker and bigger and bigger. Fear builds up inside you. And any time you want to accomplish some thing about the project, fear will be your automatic response and you will procrastinate. Know that however big it seems, your project is doable. It is possible.

Build your physical as well as mental strength. That is key to reach bigger goals.

Your health is key in your entrepreneurial journey. It helps you to achieve bigger goals. To be energetic and active throughout the day, you have to take a good care of your physical and mental strength. Entrepreneurship is demanding and you will be required to wear many hats. You will go through tough and hard moments. If you don't give your health the attention it deserves, you will be hurt.

It is not only your health that you'll put in danger. Because you will get it harder and harder to function well, your business will also fall in to jeopardy. You will face burn outs each day. Stressful days will fill your life. Your body will find it hard to function well because of exhaustion. Your mind's health will drop. It starts to fail to accomplish even simpler tasks. Its performance will decrease.

It is therefore a must that you have healthy practices for your physical and mental health. You have to develop routines that make you fit and strong. You have to do exercises that help you stay vigorous and enable you work in your full potential.

Physical strength. Your physical strength is your ticket to a healthy life style. When ever you are exercising, you are building your overall health. You are making your body adaptable. Different physical and chemical changes happen to your body. Helpful hormones are produced that strengthen your vigor. You will also be able to lead a happy and peaceful life.

You have to have a daily exercise routine therefore. Dedicate fifteen to twenty minutes a day for your physical exercise. You will notice changes in your performance and health. Your happiness also increases. The chemical change that occurs in your body will help you stay robust. The different hormones your body will be producing helps you lead a happy and interesting life.

You may hit the gym or you may do some exercises at home. There are plenty of resources on the internet. Choose routines that are suitable for you. Start small and make it a habit to exercise daily. You may find it difficult at first, but if you are determined, you will find it interesting.

Mental strength. As you do physical exercises for your physical health, your mind also needs practice to stay fit. Our brain is the master of our body. Keeping its health is therefore vital. Your memory, executive functioning abilities, creativity and happiness all depend or the health of your mind. And luckily we can train our mind. This is because our mind is capable of tremendous change.

You may challenge your brain with some practices that appeal to you. There are different exercises you may do to make your brain fit. You may learn a new language. Or you may learn musical instruments. The more challenge you give to your brain, the more fit and capable it becomes. Because our mind is elastic, it is capable of change.

You may also practice meditation. Ten to twenty minutes of meditation a day will make your mind calm and serene. Exercising gratefulness is also important. It plays a great role in rewiring your brain. Healthy practices will make your mind your loyal servant.

You need to be a life long learner if you want to succeed as a leader and an entrepreneur.

You are an entrepreneur. You have strong ambition to make difference in this world. You want to change the world. And you are the leader of that change you want to see. There is strong motive behind you, a motive that enable you to achieve greater results. This motive is a never-dying one because you are a life long learner. The light inside you gets brighter and brighter.

You always keep yourself inquisitive. There is much you can accomplish in this world. You have started the way. The more you learn, the more curious you become. Life continues to surprise you. You will forget the banalities and focus on the big picture. You will find yourself engaged and even immersed. You will love your quest. Your pursuit continues to get bigger and bigger.

This is who you are. The leader and entrepreneur you have always wanted to be. You always see change on the horizon. When you reach there, you will see nothing but another horizon. The road never stops to fill you with wonder. You may consider these to make your life filled with joy.

Read books. Books are your mentors. They show you the way. Books are your companions. They support you. Books are your friends. They fill you with excitement and happiness. If you are not accustomed to reading and want to change that, pick one book that you found the title interesting and try to read it. To make reading a habit, you have to start reading.

Talk to people. It makes you a better person to share your world views with people. Meeting new people makes you see things from different perspectives. It broadens your thinking and opens doors for different opportunities. Share what you have with friends. Network with people like you in different clubs and associations.

Master new skills. There is nothing exciting as mastering new skills. It may be a sport game or a musical instrument. You will find it interesting. The commitment you show in doing this will light on other things you do in life. You will also enjoy yourself and have so much fun.

Stay hungry. You want that drive to accomplish great things. You want that excitement that help you get to new territories. You want that joy which fills you with happiness. The solution to this is to stay hungry. Your accomplishments are greatly influenced by how much you need it. Great things happen to people who want it the most.

And there is one amazing thing about staying hungry. It gives you joy that never ends. When you achieve one thing, it opens doors to the other. It takes you from one joy to another. Stay hungry and enjoy what life is ready to give you.

Part II - Strong Leadership

They say leaders are in short supply. That seem to be the case when we see the number of failing businesses even before they stand from the ground. And although there is no a quick fix for this, mastering leadership qualities come highly recommended. With proper leadership in place, businesses are more likely to succeed.

Entrepreneurs come in different forms and so is their leadership style. Understanding one self better, nurturing your qualities and acquiring new skills is what entrepreneurs should do every day. And it is guaranteed that they are going to reap the benefits of daring to know themselves and the people they lead better.

Chapter Four - Lead me to my destiny. Who is a leader?

He or she is usually trust worthy. He or she makes things happen. Any thing he or she touches turn in to a great success. The list goes on - the qualities we may state about a good leader. We need a good leader almost in each and every things we do in life. Business is no different. It needs an outstanding leadership.

The choices and decisions the leader of a bushiness make greatly impact the success and achievement of a business. It is therefore a must that you learn leadership skills. It may seem that it is possible to achieve an overnight success. That is not the case if you take a close look at any successful business. It is the result of lots of experimentation and hardwork. It is the result of the the hardwork of leaders found at each and every level.

What type of leader are you?

It is important that you cultivate your leadership skill. The first step to start to do this is to understand your strengths and weaknesses. You may also use introspection and take some time to understand yourself. It would be very easy for you and the people you lead to know each other for better cooperation and collaboration.

You as a leader has the obligation to set your company culture. One thing is inevitable though. Not everybody is going to like what you do. Your job is to come up with the best decision. You may or may not offend others. It is good to come up with decision that will make you popular. But that is not always the case. Your decision may face strong objection.

You need to make sure that the measures you take are perfectly understood and well communicated throughout the company. The results and successes you are able to achieve will earn you respect. You don't need to aggressively enforce any thing on your people. Rather you should encourage openness and discussion at all levels. You should let everyone know that their voices matter.

Good leaders are also very god listeners. They are able to look at things from every direction and come up with excellent decision. Because they have everyone's support, they are good with people. They also take time for themselves to make sense of the decisions they made and how the future would look like. Because of their leadership skill, excellent decisions come naturally to them and they trust their gut feelings.

They have a good understanding of what is going on inside and outside their company. They are well organized and prepared. They keep their physical and mental health so as to stay active. They keep their emotions in check and stay away from the things that rob them of their stability. They prevent themselves from burnout.

They are well connected to the people they work with. They take lessons from every actions they take and every moves they make. They are able to reason out and explain things in such a way that it is easily understood by everyone.

You won't be a great leader overnight. You have to learn every day to become one. Develop this traits and work on mastering them. You will find the journey interesting and your effort is going to pay you the best rewards.

While you may not need to change who you are, adopting and learning from the traits of successful leaders will help you greatly. You have to be able to foster the leader in you. Your hardwork pays and you deserve to enjoy all the success that follow.

Work on your emotional intelligence. It will make you be in control and achieve what you want.

It is good to be talented. But it is not the only thing you need to be successful. Being emotionally intelligent has greater impact on your life. To do better at living a satisfying life, you need to work on your emotional intelligence. It will help you in your career, social life and pretty much in every thing you pursue in life. It will fill you with courage and bravery.

To master your emotional intelligence, you have to choose and follow some proven techniques. The first thing is to understand your emotions. How do you respond to any thing that happens in your life determine your emotional well being. You have to know what effect your actions have in your mood and emotional stability.

Different thoughts come to your mind every seconds. The human mind has tens of thousands of thoughts every day. You respond to some thoughts and some other thoughts pass unnoticed. The actions you take on your thoughts will form your thought patterns. If you often respond to your negative thoughts and give them power on you, this will form your thought pattern and you will develop unhealthy mood swings and stress.

Where as, if you respond to positive thoughts and choose them over negative thoughts, a positive thought pattern will develop and you will have healthy mood throughout the day. Your thoughts have no power if you don't give them the attention. It is our response to them that determine the outcome. It is therefore important that we have mastery over our thoughts.

This leads to a happier and fulfilling life. Your happiness emerges from the inside. Disregardless of conditions and circumstances, you will develop inner strength. You will see your view of the world change. Your life will be filled with positivity. You will start to see the good in people and and any thing else in life.

You will understand your environment better. Since you have developed your emotional intelligence, you won't have problem being aware of yours and peoples' emotions. Optimism takes over your life and every situation turn out to be good.

People who are emotionally intelligent are always better achievers than their peers. You as an entrepreneur have to work on your emotional intelligence. It greatly impact your success. It helps you be a better leader.

You have the power to turn difficult situation in to a better and interesting one. Your healthy and satisfying mood will embark on others and turn every conditions in to a positive one. You end up being thankful and grateful. Work on your emotional intelligence and you will reap the benefit of an over all change in your business and your life.

Leaders should be problem solvers and in fact coaches.

You just have set up a business. And you formed a team to work on a project. You took the risk and here you are, solving a problem. You have some doubt though. Your dream is big and there is something inside you that questions if it is going to happen. This doubt is very dangerous that it might grow to be a crippling problem that makes the project a failure.

This doubt must be cleared. To do that, you should demonstrate excellent leadership skill. You should be a problem solver and in fact a coach. You have to like it when employees bring their problems to you. It might not be easy, but there is nothing unsolvable. What is worse is to accumulate problem after problem and not acting up on it.

People in your team are capable of solving the problem. What they need is just collaboration and proper guidance. What you are doing is creating leaders of the future. When you solve their problem and coach them properly, you build your team as achievers of extraordinary things. So what do excellent teams need from their leader?

Support. There are times that teams get stuck because of a problem. They may find it hard to come up with solutions. Here is where they need support. And it is your job to give it to them. In fact, the problem will be easier than you thought when you act up on it. It will be solved one by one. And you will be able to draw lessons from it.

Empowerment. There is no limit as to how much people working together achieve. Leaders should be able to identify and nurture the potential of the people they lead. They should empower them and help them use their full potential.

Collaboration. Teams need collaboration to achieve greater results. You should promote and facilitate discussions and communication among the people in one team and between teams. This type of collaboration will lead you to success. Form different ways of communication throughout different levels of the company.

Employees should be team players. Leaders should make sure that team effort is valued. Conflicts should be addressed effectively and measures should be taken so that it won't happen again. The leader should always make sure that teams are performing well.

Reward. Hardwork must be celebrated. Achievements should be acknowledged. Rewarding employees who performed well and made success possible should be rewarded. This will promote a culture of discipline and determination. Leaders should acclaim high performers in different forms. Instead of being critical to them all the time, they should acknowledge the efforts and contribution of employees.

Have a discoverer's mindset and you will conquer your fear.

We know from history what early explorers did. They discovered the places that were not known to man earlier. They climbed mountains, walked on jungles, maneuvered deserts, crossed rivers and sailed overseas. The early explorers were full of strength and confidence that nothing stopped them from getting in to any territories that are not just difficult but also unthinkable.

They had to endure hunger, harsh weather, and difficult geography. They battled with wild life. Extreme conditions were not surprise but common place. Throughout their exploration, they held strong belief and great confidence in them. They conquered their fear and liberated themselves from its chain. It was only the exhilarating nature of their discovery that lead them to unchartered territories.

Having and adopting a discoverer's mindset is therefore important more than any thing to conquer your fear. Business and any thing in life for that matter, is more pleasant and appalling when we do it fearlessly and boldly. There are aspects of starting your own business that may make it hard and dangerous. You have to overcome your fear to win this limiting obstacles.

Business and exploration have so much in common. It is this nature of business that makes it interesting and wonderful. But it is also this same nature of business that makes it dreadful and terrifying. Having the mindset of a discoverer is therefore vital for you as an entrepreneur. It will make you stand tall and firm in these situations.

Difficulty. Creating your own business is not an easy task. It takes a lot of courage and hardwork to make it. Once you have decided to pursue your own business, you have to have determination and commitment all the way. You have to have similar strength that the early explorers had. You will make it happen because you are are a winner.

Uncertainty. You are not sure weather you are going to win the market or not. You are not sure weather your bold investments pay off. You are not sure if you are not going to lose. You will face uncertainty. There is a chance of losing as there is a chance of winning. In fact it is common that failures happen. A discoverer's mindset will help you stay firm in the face of uncertainty.

Rivalry. Discoverers thrived on their survival instinct. It was a live-or-die situation throughout their discovery. You will find similar conditions in your business. There is fierce competition from many competitors. A discoverer's mind set will help you win this competition by taking smart and delicate moves.

Risky. You will be in a position that you are required to take risks in business. You are seeing this amazing opportunity of growth but you are afraid you might loose. Fear is standing on your way. A discoverer's adventurous mind set will help you take the bet and enjoy its fruits. It will give you the gut that helps you win in any similar situations you are expected to take risk.

Have a beginner's mind set and you will be the driver of change.

In yoga teachings, there is one concept that every yogi, new or expert, is expected to have. That is the beginners mindset. Each and every yoga session is expected to be different and awesome. Yogis must come out of the session changed, more active and animated. Each and every session is expected to be full of wonders. And that is why every yogi is expected to have the beginner's mind set.

Business is the same. If you stop to be excited by it, if you stop the thrill, your business is going to go down the curve. Instead it favors the beginner's mind set keenly. The beginner's mind set is going to give your business life and vigor. It continues to be the source of drive for you and your company. It serves as the principle that leads your company. But why is a beginner's mindset so important?

A beginner's mind is curious. Do you remember the first day you learned to swim? You were so excited about it and you were asking so many questions. How am I going to get in to the water? How am I going to breath? How am I going to float? ... You were filled with the spirit of winning the challenge that is before you.

The same logic applies to your business. You are going to face every day with newer and newer challenges. If you approach every day with the beginner's mind set and stay curious, you will most likely win the challenges. On the other hand, if you show indifference or consider it monotonous, that is what you are going to get; a dull and stupid outcome.

A beginner's mind is energetic. You can't deny it. The first day you learned swimming is the most energetic moment you had. You were filled with this energy that made you try every routine your instructor shows you with eagerness. Time passes so fast that your first day session is over before you know it. And at the end of the session, you were asking yourself how exciting your next session will be.

Similarly, you know how energetic you felt when you first come up with your business idea and how vividly you were carrying out your plan until its launch. This is the mind set that you should have in every business endeavors that follow.

A beginner's mind is ready. After some sessions of practicing swimming, you will notice your excitement drop. You will start to be late to your training session. You may even find it hard to get out of bed and go to your training. This attitude might lead you to stop your training and quit your swimming that you were once so excited about.

Where as, if you continue to have the beginners mind set every day, you will be ready to face new challenges. You will be ready to work hard and practice. In fact you will continue to love it even more. Similarly, in your business, your execution ability grows when you have the beginner's mind set. You won't procrastinate. Rather you always get things done and take the next leap.

A beginner's mind is open. You now can swim. Thanks to your courage and your instructor's help. But still you want to learn more. You want to master other swimming techniques. Your mind is open because you held the beginners mind set.

Jeff Bezos, the founder and CEO of Amazon, is said to have this mind set. He still starts his days with the beginners mind set. When you adopt this mindset and stay open, you will be able to make your company strong and successful.

Chapter Five - The role of outstanding leadership in successful businesses. Impactful Leadership.

Businesses fail. It is common place that new businesses find it hard to flourish easily. But failures also teach you an invaluable lesson. You have to stay out of limiting traps and difficulties and take lessons from what they have to teach. You have to stay strong and learn fast from them. If you learn from your failures, they will serve you as cornerstones to the growth of your company.

You might find it hard to persevere. You may find it hard to hold on. But, your hardwork and effort is going to pay back. It is not far since your efforts come to fruition. Just stay strong that moments you have to endure the toughness of pursuing your business and you will reap the benefits. If you apply the principles of outstanding leadership, you business will most likely be a business which will impact the lives of so many.

It's human to try and fail. It is yet angelic to fail and learn.

We know that successful people are not different. They are stronger for a bit longer than we most are. They have seen the not-so-likable path that endurance and audacity require. They have went through the not-so-favorable path that persistence and perseverance need. They have seen unexpected out comes ruin what they have built for years.

They have seen failure hit. They have seen it hit harder. They have suffered its damage. They have suffered its consequences. Yet, it is their unshakable strength that won. It is their belief that sustained. They failed and learned. They came out stronger. What do we learn from these people? How can we turn our most frightening moments in to our most glaring ones?

There are times you might be caught up in confusion about yourself. You might wonder where you fit in. It is especially common in times of shortcomings to question oneself. There is nothing like failure that fuels such kind of thoughts.

You may also fall in to self-doubt. You may feel insecure about yourself. You may look yourself in the mirror of your incapabilities. Very little things will over power you. You will start to belittle yourself. You just can't stop being hard on yourself. There is nothing damaging as these kinds of thoughts.

To be successful, you need to start to view yourself in a completely different direction. You need to learn self-compassion and start to treat yourself with tenderness. One way you might do this is by treating yourself how a beloved friend might treat you. The next time you catch yourself treating yourself badly, ask *'would my friend treat me like this?'*. Show compassion for yourself and that will make the difference.

This will also help if you have self limiting beliefs. It will give you the power to unlock your amazing gift and talent. Getting rid of the self limiting beliefs you have on yourself will do wonders in your life. Treating yourself with respect and compassion rewires your brains to have strong belief in yourself. Try to read the biographies of successful people you admire. Try to learn from their story and stay as motivated as you can. Look for books that teach you life skills and power you up.

Accept yourself as a capable, loving, wonderful human being and build on this. Your self-acceptance will make a big difference. It will open doors to understand yourself better. Then build on your self-awareness. Know your likes and dislikes. Know your preferences and favorites. Know what terrifies you and makes you happy.

Your self-awareness serves you as a source of happiness and strength. In all the difficult moments and mishaps you face in life, you will stand untroubled because you have come to know nothing has power to rob you of your inner peace and stability.

You don't delegate means you are not a leader.

There is no a leader without a follower. And followers aren't doing any thing means there is no delegation. There is no delegation means you are not leading. It turns out that leaders do nothing but delegate. Successful leaders spend most of their time building a system on how delegation happens throughout the hierarchy of their company. This makes accountability a sure thing to happen.

Employees are happy when they get the recognition of the leader. This can't happen if the leader is not satisfied with the job done. This usually happens when the employee is not clear with the job he or she should do. This is the problem of the leader not the employee. The leader should be very clear or at least be open about what he or she wants to happen.

What delegation isn't. Deligation is not a time waster. Leaders deligate because they want to achieve some thing. Therefore they should be careful about following up the employees if they are on the right track. Delegation for the sake of delegation is a bad signal that the company culture is at risk.

Deligation is not a power isssue either. Leaders shouldn't deligate to show control and dominance on the employee. Cramming the employee with lots of tasks makes the project below standard and the employee unappreciated.

A company running like this end up with employees who are either rebellions or passive-aggressors.

Deligation combined with trust takes the company forawrd. Leaders should trust the employees they delligate. They should be honest with their order and generous with their support. Unexperienced leaders are usually not good with deligation. They are reserved or afraid to delegate. This lags the projects you do. That is why delegation is a quality good leaders should have and nurture.

Delegation buys time to the leader. Leading is a very important job. But it may come a very stressful thing to bear. Weather it is a small business or a very large one, weather you own the company or you're employed, you should have the right leadership skill. Delegation is one of these skills. Delegating the right way buys a good deal of time for the leader to think about important and strategic matters. It also makes the work-life balance of the leader a proper one.

It will be a choice between achievement and over-achievement. Companies usually consider jobs a high expenditure. Leaders are not few that focus on job cuts as a main profit maximizing strategy. It's correct that leaders should be very careful on hiring the right person and utilize the talent effectively. Stuffing the company with too many employees doesn't make the company any more successful or the projects any more better.

With a company well stuffed, delegation is a sure way that all important things are well taken care. The leader should focus on facilitating communication between subordinates and team leaders. And employees should be creative about their job and seek the proper guidance. All these things considered it will be a choice between only achievement or over achievement.

Procedures should determine killer systems not fatal bureaucracy for your business.

Any thing smart and beautiful in life is built from systems working together. Our very life is a system of subsystems that work in harmony. Systems give what you do structure. Systems enable you achieve your goal in simplistic and easy manner. It is this similar role that they have in your business. They make sure that each and every detail is well taken care.

Procedures make up systems. You have procedures for your core business, human resources, finances and other tasks you do at your company. Unless you make your procedures clear and simplistic, they will form fatal bureaucracy, instead of killer systems for your business. You have to take a detail look at the procedures that form your system.

Keep them simple. When you set up a working procedure, try to keep it as simple as you can. Have brainstorming sessions with employees in the department and in the departments it works with. Put every detail in paper. Come up with ways of solving its complexity. Design standard formats and papers that make communication simpler and your work easily achievable.

Make it easy to scale up. Problematic procedures can easily pose problems when companies scale up. If the procedures are not designed the growth of the company in mind, they will end up a collection of rules that only exist to make things complicated. Procedures should take care of every detail of the company's work, but they should also be designed in simpler and simpler ways.

Don't open door for clutter. Bureaucracy is born from clutter. When a procedure is not well developed from the very beginning, it usually develops in to more complicated and hard to understand one. When you need to change or improve procedures, make it in such a way that it doesn't ruin the existing system but that perfectly and easily fits to the existing one.

And don't allow too much hierarchy in your system. One way of putting unnecessary procedure in the things you do is to lengthen the hierarchy and the chain of command it requires to make it done. Keep the people involved to the minimum as possible as you can.

Make it robust. The strength of a company is measured by the strength of its systems. If you make your procedures and systems strong, it is reflected in each and every thing the company does. It will serve as a symbol of the company.

We know MacDonald and its success in building a robust system throughout the company. The value of the company and the discipline it instilled in its employees is reflected in each and every thing they do. This is what you notice in each and every MacDonald shop found in every major city around the world.

Don't whine about trying times because your business is going to turn a success shortly.

Who a successful man has ever achieved a big thing without hustling and sweating. Some achievers are even said to pass through hundreds of failures and trying times. No big thing can be achieved without experimenting and patience.

Our natural reaction to hustles and failures determine our future success. Most people stop pursuing their dreams after just one or two trials. That is why it is said *'Successful people are no stronger, they are just strong a few minutes more'*.

Strength is built from perseverance and resilience. That is the way to success. Some people chose whining over trying workable solutions. There is a tendency to call successful people lucky and claim that it's only luck which brought them there. But that is not the case. There are some points we should bear in our mind to get to know how successful people are wired.

Whining is for losers. Have you ever came across whiners. You can't feel motivated around them. The emotional burden they instill on themselves and others is very unbearable. It stops them and people around them from pursuing their dreams. Their mind is wired to pity themselves and others for their failure.

Whiners are usually losers. They don't have strength to persevere through even little problems they face. And whining is the enemy of success. Instead of filling one self with courage and motivation, whining makes you cry for excuses.

The way to success is not quitting. But whining is so undesirable that it makes you quit the passion you have for yourself. Businesses succeed after a well tought idea and a tremendous courage. Whining is the enemy of this. You are willing to pay every price the success of your business needs means you are at the path of a big achievement.

Trying times. No a man or a woman has achieved great things without hustling and trying times. Your suffering and working hard are the source of your future success. You drew lots of important lessons out of them. You should love your trying times and the strength the success you want to enjoy require.

The hardest moments and times you have to endure are the base of your success. You have to persevere and do what is expected of you to achieve great success. Success doesn't happen over night. It requires a lot of resilience. It needs to take responsibility for each and every thing that happens to your life, the good and the bad.

There is one thing that sums every thing you have to pass through before you succeed. Loving the process. To reach the point where you dreamed, you have to love the process - the hardships you have to pass through - the difficult moments that took you closer to giving up. It is after all these things that the success you achieved come meaningful and pleasant.

This signals a success. You achieved a lot no matter what. You have never give the slightest of chance for yourself to give up. Lots of people admire the strength you have and that you came attain. Every one admires your strength. Your ability to look for solutions in the very hardest of problems serve yourself and others as a motivation.

What else can signal a success other than this. Success is easily achievable for determined and committed people. That is why we celebrate and learn from successful people the world has given us. The energy and passion they have for their job and the love and enthusiasm they have for what they do is contagious.

Successful people do understand the power of their imagination and goal. They never doubt its ability to bring forth change to people's lives. They know they can't escape from failure in the process. Therefore, they try to change every undesirable situation in to things they could take a lesson from.

Sustainable success is what we need. All the great successful men and women that we saw in history and we see today have one thing in common. They are not quitters. The change they want to see in the world derived them and enabled them achieve the extraordinary success that we admire today.

Sustainable success is achieved through sustainable hardwork. If you adhere to this mind set, success is a sure thing to happen and in fact it is going to happen shortly. If you want to entertain success in your life, what you must be doing is do what you do with determination and commitment. Success surely follows.

To make our success sustainable, we have to take charge of everything we do. Every decisions we make and every actions we take determine what we get. We therefore need to patiently and strongly adhere to what we do to make changes to our life and business.

Success is tricky. There is a chance that you are already successful although it doesn't feel like it. Success is tricky. What people consider a success is different from people to people. For some people it is financial success. For others it is mastering something in their field. And yet it is another thing for others.

That is why success is tricky. And sooner or later you are going to come across a setback. What defines true success is the ability to pass through setbacks. That is why having a goal and purpose in life and achieving them, or being in the process is considered a success.

Success is tricky if you don't know what you want. Have a clear idea about what you want to achieve. You might get something else and consider that a success when you don't have a clear idea of what you want. That will not only leave you unsatisfied, but it also leave what you want unachieved.

How to tell if your business is on the right track? These are signs you are succeeding against the odds.

You have walked the step. You have passed the hurdles of starting your own business and you are up and running.

How can you tell if you are on the right track? What shows that you are succeeding? You can't tell for sure the success of your business in few months of your launch. Customers are going to take some time to get know what you provided for them.

But the market always sends some signals and you have to pick up on them. To start to notice and make adjustments early on is one good practice for a successful business. Building up on each and every small successes you get is a necessary step you should take. Results are going to accrue and you will start to notice big changes.

Customers are starting to love you. One good sign that shows your business is succeeding is that customers are in fact starting to respond. They have noticed your hardwork and how you wanted to talk to them. They are starting to understand what actually you are going to provide them. They are in fact starting to love you.

You are starting to be noticed. Your business is gaining traction and you are starting to be noticed. The good work you put up on your products and services is catching the eye of many. You are starting to appear in some blogs and media out lets. People are sharing and liking you on social media. They are tweeting and talking about your products.

There is a high potential for growth. The other most important thing that shows your business is succeeding is that you are seeing a high potential for growth. Looking at your customers response so far, you are able to see that the products you brought to your customers are in fact very much needed and you responded to a very potential market.

You are gaining some insight in to how you will be serving your customers better. You are understanding what exactly your customers needs are and how you are going to be able to satisfy them. You are seeing a bright future for your business.

You are gaining confidence. And this all is teaching you something. This is teaching you that success is on the verge. You are gaining confidence that your business is not just working but also succeeding. You are gaining coincidence that your business is not just providing customers with some thing usable, but also some thing lovable.

Building up on this confidence and listening to your customers, you will be able to grow your company to a better and larger one. Because your products are great and your services are great, your company is going to turn up a success against all odds.

You will enjoy life as an entrepreneur as you would enjoy your holiday trip.

You have shaped what the road ahead looks like. Surprises await. You should never stop to be thrilled by the wonders of getting in to and staying in business. Your entrepreneurial endeavor needs life. Besides the hardwork you put in, you need to bring in new energy and motivation. Your business shouldn't fall short of inspirations in any way.

Get in to deeper conversations with your friends. Share your world views openly. This broadens your personal knowledge and interpersonal relationships. Get out of your comfort zone and try new things you haven't tired before. When you go to restaurants, have new food from the menu and listen to the kinds of music you don't listen much often.

Dedicate some time for vacation. You may set a vacation every six months. Go out and visit the places you find interesting. Connect to nature more often. This will give you the disconnect and refreshment you need. Use your weekend to do tasks that are out of your day to day activities. Meet and start your week with a refreshed and energized mind.

An energized mind is healthier and highly functional. It helps you to be more creative and imaginative. It prevents you from burn outs and stresses. It will make you more organized and well managed in your every activities.

You will have a flawless working time. You will be in your flow state most often and find yourself wondering how fast time passed. You will accomplish tasks before deadlines and will have plenty of time to plan and organize.

Read books. They widen your knowledge and even help you live longer. Readers are said to live longer than non-readers. Challenge yourself by learning newer skills. You will develop strong imaginative power.

Meditate regularly. Meditation has excellent and proven health benefits. It reduces the size of our brain part which is found at the back called amygdala. It is related with the fight and flight response. It is also related with fear. Its reduced size means you will have mastery over your fear.

Meditation is also know to increase our prefrontal cortex, the front part of our mind. It is related with executive functioning. It will help you have excellent organization and executing capabilities. Another benefit of meditation is that it increases the grey matter found in our brain. Integrate meditation in your daily routines for a better and sustained results.

Having the life style you want, and integrating that in to your life will give you a happy and fulfilling life. Because it is filled with wonders and amusements, you will enjoy life as an entrepreneur as you would enjoy your holiday trip.

Part III - Vibrant Economy

We tend to believe that human nature is changed, getting greedier than ever. We say humanity is getting worse, because people are getting materialistic than ever. We claim that the new generation is getting hopeless, because the world is being filled with lots of problems than ever. Me, I say all this is a fuss and want to claim that humanity is evolving.

The gap we see between the riches and the poor, the unfortunate deaths and sufferings we witness day in and day out, the unfulfilled wishes and necessities we disregard, all these are homeworks for every one of us. We need to work toward addressing the societal divide and answer the questions that need to be answered.

Chapter Six - He who defines the Economy. Economies aren't to be understood, they are to be defined.

Entrepreneurs should be the drivers of change not the followers of it. They should lead the road ahead for a better and prosperous world. The lives of so many people in Africa who live below poverty line, the futures of so many people in war torn regions of the world which is put at risk; these are assignments to us all and young entrepreneurs of the world in particular.

Economic prosperity should be the focus of the policies and procedures we put forth for a better and developed world. It should be the first priority for a peaceful and advanced world. And the youth have both responsibility and choice to make it so.

Prosperity is a choice. Why aren't some countries rich anyway? Civilization is a right. Why aren't some countries still civilized anyway?

There are lots of countries which pride themselves for their amazing history and culture. There are lots of ancient civilizations that are found world wide. As unique and amazing their history is, they haven't enjoyed the wealth and prestige they deserve. Many of them are torn by the civil wars the countries went through, and there is a lack of well evolved political system that wasn't able to sustain more than few decades. It made the countries lag behind many of their counterparts. Their flawed political systems have also shadowed their economy. Although many are among the fastest growing economies, it is very hard to say that they have positioned themselves well in the ever changing and competition driven world.

The make up and structure of their economy lacks competence. The unemployment rate, the incompetent financial institutions which run their economy, the policies that govern it, and the unstructured business practices that need attention are its multi-faceted problems. Many of the endeavors these countries carried out for a better economy haven't lead to fruition because it seems that they are sweating the small staff.

In the capitalist world we live in, the rich are getting richer, and the poor are getting poorer. Although prosperity is a right given to us all, they don't seem to get it right. Especially in developing countries, there exists a big class difference, and all fights to eliminate it seem to fail. What are they missing?

Wealth begets wealth. Their political system should be competent. Being trapped in a vicious circle of civil wars that emanate from racial and cultural differences and, poverty and backwardness which are attributed to lack of proper leadership must be addressed.

Their economic system should align itself with the rest of the world. Fellow men and women should think and speak wealth. Work toward reducing the number of the poor should be done. Young entrepreneurs and business owners should be supported to create more jobs for a better economy. The ultimate goal should be to come out of the devastating poverty.

This is only possible if all parts of the community work toward wealth. The rich should preach toward wealth. The middle class should align themselves toward wealth. The poor should push toward wealth. This is the only way out of the catch 22 they are in.

So what is the takeaway?

It proves we don't ruin the few leaps we were able to make. Following the *'Wealth Begets Wealth'* motto makes sure that the few leaps we were able to make so far are not ruined and lost. Most of the political systems that govern the today's world are tested over the long history of these countries. It seems that it's more of a damage than a reward they got from most of it. The control the politics had on their economy also made it lag behind. But it is always never too late to learn from mistakes. We should address the problems in both the political and economic systems.

It makes our goal approachable and attainable. Poverty seems to be the root for all the complex problems these countries are in. To make the goal approachable and attainable, we should make the race only for a better and prosperous world. Nurturing entrepreneurial spirit and culture and instilling it among the youth will prove itself right in solving all the major problems we face.

It makes prosperity and civilization come second nature to these people. Prosperity and Civilization seem very strange for most of the citizens of these countires. The path to it doesn't seem to be well defined and engineered. The youth seem to not know what to do, the adult seem to be lost and the elders seem to be exhausted. It is only by helping them take charge and empower them to work toward determining their own destiny that they will be able to bring and attract wealth to themselves and their nation.

It makes it clear and obvious that our entrepreneurs are brave and smart enough to achieve it. The *'Wealth Begets Wealth'* mantra is what drives a prosperous economy. Entrepreneurs should be able to aspire and achieve impactful changes in their community and else where in the world. This can only happen if they get all the support they need from all stake holders. To make movers and shakers of the economy brave and smart enough, we need to form a well articulated economic system.

Epilogue

Entrepreneurs, as the creators of impactful businesses and enterprises, should get all the support they need from family, friends, other businesses and the government. All taken care, the success of the business and the change it brings to people's lives is the measure of the success of the entrepreneur.

Entrepreneurs should learn from successful business leaders both in their own and other industries. They should develop a network of peers and mentors as well as partners and advisers. They also need to learn about the business they lead and the skills it requires every day. They should also gain insight from books and other resources they find helpful.

I am sure this book provided one. I am very interested in listening to your comments, there fore. What does your entrepreneurial pursuit look like? What story would you like to share? How were you able to impress the world with the business you created? Please email me at *semuashenafi@gmail.com*.